Angels can fly
because they take themselves lightly.

G. K. CHESTERTON

[handwritten inscription:]

1/98

Rex/Barbara—

Blessings & joy in the Lord! Great to have you & your wife with us — She's great.

Rich Bimler

ANGELS CAN FLY
BECAUSE THEY TAKE THEMSELVES LIGHTLY

How to Keep Happy and Healthy
as a Person of God

RICHARD BIMLER

CPH
SAINT LOUIS

Copyright © 1992 Concordia Publishing House
3558 S. Jefferson Avenue, St. Louis, MO 63118–3968
Manufactured in the United States of America

Library of Congress Cataloging-in-Publication Data

Bimler, Richard.
   Angels can fly because they take themselves lightly / Richard Bimler.
   ISBN 0-570-04577-0
   1. Church work—Lutheran Church. 2. Church work—Humor.
3. Lutheran Church—Anecdotes.   I. Title.
BV4400.B55   1992
248.8′9—dc20   92-8586

   3 4 5 6 7 8 9 10   VP   01 00 99 98 97 96 95

To Matthew Richard Cillick,
my grandson number one,
whose joy and celebration of life
help to make me fly

CONTENTS

ABOUT
THIS BOOK

The stories and reflections included here are intended to assist us in

• affirming that we have a happy God;

• modeling what it means to be joyful in the Lord;

• helping us lighten up and not take ourselves too seriously;

• encouraging the sharing of hope and joy intentionally with each other;

• giving us hooks on which to hang our happiness in the Lord, starting at the cross and the empty tomb.

Enjoy these pages with me as we find ourselves chuckling a little and sharing these stories with others, all in the spirit of joy and hope in our Lord, who loves us and who loves to laugh with us!

RICH BIMLER

AS YOU BEGIN

This is a book of celebrations. It should be a fun book to read, because it doesn't take itself so seriously. Its purpose is to help you affirm and enjoy your faith in the Lord Jesus. It is intended to help you rejoice in the promise of new life in Jesus Christ as a given. All of our joy and celebration grows out of that fact. Christ has already done it all for us. It is finished. He has had the last laugh over the devil. His death and resurrection have given us the victory!

Our purpose in life is to celebrate Christ's presence among us. And as we do this, we are enabled to take ourselves lightly because we know very seriously that the Lord Jesus Christ is the Lord of our lives. And that's something to shout and sing and fly about.

I am reminded of the little girl attempting to recite Psalm 23. She said, "The Lord is my Shepherd. That's all I want!" And that's all we need also. The little girl was correct. The Lord is ours. He has paid the price for our sins. We are free to celebrate the gift of life that is ours. Hooray and Amen!

The flight plan for our journey through these pages will focus on various parts of the Christian life and faith. I will be sharing stories and encouraging you to think and add your own stories as well. I will be providing you with opportunities to reflect on your Christian lifestyle and to develop more of a pro-active, joyful approach to life. Each section includes thoughts and reflections which may be of help to you in your celebrative life.

You may want to jump around throughout these pages, focusing on a certain section on certain days of your life. This is one book you do not need to read page by page in sequence. And that's just another way of modeling that our lives in the Lord can be creative and spontaneous.

And now, let's get on with the celebration!

ABOUT
THE TITLE

It was G.K. Chesterton who first wrote, "Angels can fly because they take themselves lightly. Never forget that Satan fell by force of gravity."

It seemed appropriate to title this book "Angels Can Fly Because They Take Themselves Lightly," with due credit to G. K.—which probably stands for Genial and Kind—in order to emphasize the fact that people of God have the power to celebrate and fly to new heights. And we can do it because of what Christ did that first Easter Sunday.

So often you and I get caught up in the humdrum problems and frustrations of life. Yes, they are real, and they are constantly present. But we can fly because of Christ's death and resurrection. That's our power. That's our joy!

Two caterpillars were crawling along one day. One of them spotted a butterfly soaring joyfully overhead. It remarked to the other caterpillar, "You'll never catch me in one of those things!" And that's just the problem. You and I have been cleared for takeoff, but so often we just sit on the runway, reflecting and worrying and pondering our flight plan.

He has risen! We are free to fly to new heights!
Look out world, here we come!

THE ART
OF HAPPYING

A little boy was asked by his teacher, "What do you want to be when you grow up?"

He replied, "Happy!"

You and I are called by God to be happy. And He provides this lifestyle by sending His Son to die and rise for us. To be happy does not mean that everything has to go right, and that problems and frustrations disappear. Instead, being happy in the Lord means that, because of His presence, we continue to be connected with the knowledge of His joy and forgiveness, even as we struggle through our pains and problems in life. A happy person in the Lord is one who knows from where strength and comfort come.

The Sermon on the Mount is an excellent model of happying. Our Lord calls his people "blessed," or "happy," and says, "Be happy and glad, for a great reward is kept for you in heaven."

Reflections

1. Who in your life helps to make you happy? How?

2. Who do you help make happy? How?

3. Who in your life needs the gift of happying right now? How can you supply that gift?

CALL ME LUCKY

The story is often told of a lost-and-found item in the newspaper that reads like this:

Lost Dog

3 legs. Blind in left eye. Missing right ear. Tail broken. Recently hit by a truck. Answers to the name Lucky.

Have you ever felt that way? I have! And yet, isn't it super that our Lord still calls us lucky? Because of our Baptism and His love and forgiveness, we are the lucky ones as God continues to pour His blessings upon us.

And now it is our task to go out and tell others how lucky they are to have a Lord who refreshes, renews, and forgives.

Just call me lucky!

Reflections

1. When do you most often feel lucky? Why?

2. Who needs some words of forgiveness and comfort right now, maybe even from you?

JOY IN THE MIDST OF REALITY

Recent statistics from the Children's Defense Fund state that every day in the United States

- 7,742 teenagers become sexually active.
- 2,795 teenagers get pregnant.
- 67 babies die before one month of life.
- 27 children die from poverty.
- 6 teenagers commit suicide.
- 135,000 children bring a gun to school.
- 211 children are arrested for drug abuse.
- 1,512 teenagers drop out of school.
- 3,288 children run away from home.
- 34,286 people lose jobs.
- 1,849 children are abused or neglected.
- . . . and on and on and on.

And I say that we should be happy and rejoice? That's right! The Lord has empowered us to reach out to these people with the love and care that He first has given to us. He has equipped us to make a difference in people's lives by first putting us right with Himself, through the death and resurrection of Jesus.

Romans 5:10–11 says it well, "We were God's enemies, but He made us His friends through the death of His Son. . . . But that is not all; we rejoice because of what God has done through our

Lord Jesus Christ."

More Good News to share is that the Lord has freed us from having to worry about ourselves in terms of our relationship with Him. He has assured us of our salvation in Christ. Our faith is a gift from Him! And that allows us to turn our energies to sharing that love and forgiveness with other people, who do not yet know the joy that is ours, and can be theirs!

Reflections

1. How can you share the joy of the Lord with someone hurting and troubled today?

2. What would you say to a person who is not joyful in the Lord?

YOU ARE SPECIAL

David says it so well, "You created my inmost being; you knit me together in my mother's womb. I praise you because I am fearfully and wonderfully made" (Ps. 139:13–14 NIV).

And it's true. Isn't it great that the Lord did not put any conditions on His loving us! He did not say "you are wonderfully made—if you run three miles every day and eat only the most healthy foods," or "if your family always agrees on things and never argues," or "if your life is in perfect condition and everyone smiles all the time." No, He states the fact that you and I have been miraculously made—and we are His forever. Isaiah 43:1 gets into the act and even states that the Lord calls us by name—we are His.

Wow, what a lift! What a joy to know this fact when we are struggling with the problems of life. What an assurance that we have a Lord who loves and forgives and comforts us. And that's something we can share with others too!

Reflections

1. Are there specific times when you do not feel "wonderfully made"? What comfort do you find in God's Word?

2. Who needs a word of comfort today? How can you share your joy in the Lord with this person? Go for it!

THE BIBLE AS A JOY BOOK

The word joy is used almost 200 times in the Scriptures. The Lord often counseled and comforted His friends by saying, "Be of good cheer."

Laughter is mentioned in the Bible about 50 times. Elton Trueblood, in *The Humor of Christ*, (Harper and Row, 1964), states, "We do not know with certainty how much humor there is in Christ's teaching, but we can be sure there is far more than is normally recognized." Someone else put it this way, "If you want to know if God has a sense of humor, just look in the mirror!"

Our joy and laughter begin at the cross where we see God taking our sin upon Himself in order to turn our sorrow into joy. The joy in our lives comes from knowing that the Lord has taken away our grief and sin and given us a new joy in Him!

Our joy begins quietly at the cross and builds to Easter! And Easter becomes every day as we live out our lives as Resurrection Resources! The message is loud and clear: Our joy exults at Easter and flows into all of life.

Reflections

1. What in your life tends to take away your joy in the Lord?

2. Ask friends and family members the same question and discuss how you can help each other in reflecting the joy of the Lord.

PORTRAIT OF A LAUGHING JESUS

Lois Morgan shares her gift of poetry in *The Joyful Noiseletter*, Fellowship of Merry Christians, Kalamazoo, MI:

Jesus,
I believe you laughed as Mary bathed you

And Joseph tickled your toes.
I believe you giggled as you and other children
Played your neighborhood games.
And when you went to the temple and as-
   tounded the teachers,
I believe you chuckled as all children chuckle
when they stump adults.
And surely there were moments of merriment
   as you and your
Disciples depthed your relationship.
And as you and Mary and Martha and Lazarus
   fellowshipped,
Mirth must have been mirrored on your faces.
Jesus, I know you wept and anguished.
But I believe you laughed too.
Create in me
The life of laughter.

Reflections

1. Look in the Scriptures for other times you think Jesus laughed and shared humor.

2. Write a prayer/poem reflecting your faith, your humor, your thoughts regarding the Lord of faith and humor. Share it with someone special.

IF YOU LOVE JESUS

If you love Jesus, why not tell your face about it?

This is one of my favorite sayings. It captures

the gap between what we say about our faith and how we live it out. It points to our humanness, and therefore to the need for humor in our lives.

This does not mean that we walk around laughing and guffawing, oblivious to the pains and hurts in our lives. It does mean, however, that the love of the Lord is what allows us to live out a life joy-filled and celebrative.

Do you know anyone who is always smiling? Kind of makes you sick, doesn't it? In the words of Martin Luther (a loose translation!), the only way to get up every morning with a smile on your face is to go to bed every night with a coat hanger in your mouth! And we surely do not want to do that!

And so we smile, we laugh, we celebrate, in spite of it all! Because we have the last laugh— Christ's victory over death. And sometimes, those of us of German ancestry, as I am, need to be taught the gift of smiling and laughing. I'm reminded of the story of the German husband, married over 40 years, who loved his wife so much that he almost told her!

Maybe we Germans need to be more like "joy-mans"!

Reflections

1. Try smiling at people today. See what kind of reactions you receive!

2. Discuss with others reasons for laughing and smiling. See how they are similar and different.

BEING HUMAN IS BEING HUMOROUS

I firmly believe that everyone has a sense of humor. Some have special gifts as storytellers, some as joke tellers, but all of us have been given the gift of humor. It just depends on how we choose to use it.

Check it out for yourself: do you know anyone whom you think has no sense of humor whatsoever? I used to think that of John. John always seemed to be serious, sober, never smiling, and at times, came close to being called a grouch. But then I saw him playing with his grandkids. Wow, was he funny! And his grandkids certainly knew that they have a happy grandpa!

Being human is being humorous. It involves not taking yourself so seriously. It is knowing that we will goof things up, and knowing that the Lord still loves and forgives, and gives us another chance. This condition of ours (called sin) continues to focus us back to the cross and the empty tomb for our strength, our purpose, our joy!

God's people raised their voices in celebration of God's grace in Psalm 126:1–3: "When the Lord brought us back to Jerusalem, it was like a dream! How we laughed, how we sang for joy! Then the other nations said about us, 'The Lord did great things for them.' Indeed he did great things for us; how happy we were!"

And that's good enough for me!

Reflections

1. Think of that one person who seems to be lacking humor. Go share your joy with that person.

2. Search the Scriptures for other examples of people sharing their joy and sense of humor in the Lord.

DYING OR LIVING

A friend of mine recently shared this story of life with me. She was discussing the fact that a friend had been diagnosed as having terminal cancer. She visited her to cheer her up and, hopefully, help her cope with the illness. What happened was exactly the opposite.

Upon arrival at the hospital, she was greeted with a pleasant "Hi" from the patient. After some informal chatting, the visitor asked what she could do. The patient simply smiled and said, "One thing. Please tell people one thing about me. Tell them that I am not dying of cancer. Tell them that I am *living* with cancer!"

And my friend says she has seen life from a different perspective ever since that day!

Are we dying, or are we living, with whatever diseases we have—cancer, family turmoil, failures at work, insufficient time, broken dreams, heartaches? I don't mean to imply that we should deny our pain and suffering, but rather deal with it on the basis of Christ's death and resurrection for us!

We all deal with the symptoms of sin and death each day. That's reality. And it hurts. And we all deal with life each day also. And that's the joy and the hope and the promise which the Lord gives us!

"But thanks be to God who gives us the victory through our Lord Jesus Christ" (1 Cor. 15:57).

Reflections

1. How can you share the joy of living today with someone who needs to hear Christ's hope and comfort?

2. Review St. Paul's letters and note how often he refers to living and dying—in the Lord.

I RESIGN!

A friend of mine claims that each night when he goes to bed he says to the Lord, "Lord, I resign! That's it. I give up. Life is too hard. I've had it!"

Then, as his story goes, if he wakes up the next morning, that must mean that the Lord

hasn't accepted his resignation!

What a celebrative way to live! To see each day as a new gift from the Lord. And to rejoice in the words of Lamentations 3:23–24, "Fresh as the morning, as sure as the sunrise. The Lord is all I have, and so I put in Him my hope."

Have you ever felt like resigning? Me too! What is it that keeps us going? I would suggest that it is knowing that our Lord continues to love and forgive and care for us. He loves us now and forever, and that fact will never change. We are also comforted and built up by others saying this to us, and showing us His love through words and actions.

I'm not okay. You're not okay. But God says, "That's okay"!

Life is for giving! Because we are forgiven!

Reflections

1. Choose someone this day and speak a word of affirmation and hope.
2. Ask a special person around you to speak words of peace and joy to you, especially on days when you need that love and care.

KEEPING HEALTHY AND HAPPY

True story: I once had to cancel a conference workshop when I became ill with a flu bug. The topic I was to discuss was: How to Keep Happy and Healthy as a Professional Church Worker! Yes, the truth hurts. And so do times when we are not able to follow through on our assignments and responsibilities. But, there still is hope!

I'm convinced that the Lord continues to keep us humble and honest by giving us opportunities that force us to rely on Him and His promises. Whenever we become so self-sufficient, so professional, so "I've-got-it-all-together," He comes with His loving hand and helps us to keep things in perspective.

Our health and happiness do come from the Lord. Sure, He gives us wisdom to take care of our bodies and monitor what we eat and drink, and how we exercise. But none of this replaces our reliance on the Lord for our health and wellness.

I'm reminded of the runner whose running became his god. So much in fact that he didn't have time for church or family or anything else. He became a running addict, until one day he was struck by a car. He now claims that this was the best accident that ever happened to him. And he still runs, although he's not as possessed with running as before. And he runs on less-busy streets!

Reflections

1. Is there anything in your life that is possessing you and may need to be evaluated?
2. Discuss this same question with a close friend and see how you can help each other.

LAUGHTER

God created us with a great capacity for laughter. What a gift! What a blessing! Dr. John Strelan, from Australia, makes the scriptural connection for us:

Dear old Sarah.
At least she had a sense of humor
and she knew the difference
between law and promise:
between the law of genetics and
the promise of God.
She couldn't for the life of her see
how the distance
between the two could be bridged—
So she laughed . . .

. . . and laughed and laughed when
God gave life to her empty womb and
she birthed her baby boy.
Isaac: Laughter, she called him
just to remind herself of
God's loving greatness and
her own laughter.

If God's promise to bring forth life
from a dead womb
made Sarah laugh out loud,
how much more does what God did for us
raise in us great shouts
of laughter.

God gave life to His Son, dead in the tomb.

Laugh, then, for all you are worth!
For through that risen Son you have life:
Life filled with purpose, hope, and
—despite the pain, the tears—
laughter.

Reflections

1. Think of other scriptural stories that show joy and humor.
2. Look over the life of Jesus in the Gospels and pinpoint some times of laughter and joy.

DEAD SERIOUSNESS OR SERIOUS JOYFULNESS?

Some people are dying of dead seriousness! I'd rather be serious about joyfulness. Granted, there can be a thin line between joy and humor and silliness. Humor can be misused and abused just as much as any other gift.

But why be so serious about life anyway? No one is going to get out of it alive! People of God, you and me, need to enable each other to create a positive mindset about life. Life—it's a gift from God. And like all other gifts, we accept it and use it to its fullest.

Sometimes I really take myself too seriously—my job, my responsibilities, my family, myself.

And when I do, I lose the focus on living a joy-filled life for other people. I major in minors and minor in majors. I cause stress for myself and others because I still attempt to do it all myself, and in my own way.

Remembering when our own kids were growing up, I uncomfortably recall the many times my agenda was not the most helpful or positive.

● We finally made it to Old Faithful at Yellowstone National Park after many days of travel, and I didn't want to take the time to wait for it to gush!

● I would continue to harp at my son Mike to clean his room, instead of spending time with him, talking about faith and hopes and dreams. (We did finally agree that he would rake his room once a month!)

● I was too busy doing the "work of the Lord" to spend time at home with my wife Hazel, and Diane, Bob, and Mike.

The joy in all of this is that you and I are provided the ministry opportunities to continue to live and love in Jesus' name as we live joyfully forgiven.

Reflections

1. Recall a time when you became dead serious about something that didn't call for such a drastic reaction.

2. Review the past week and evaluate how much joy and how much seriousness your schedule has provided you.

IF I HAD IT
TO DO OVER

The following article is adapted from "Be Happy" written in 1989 by an 85-year-old man who learned that he was dying.

If I had my life to live over, I'd try to make more mistakes next time. I wouldn't be so perfect. I would relax more. I'd limber up. I'd be sillier than I've been on this trip. In fact, I know very few things that I would take so seriously. I'd be crazier, I'd be less hygienic.

I'd take more chances; I'd take more trips; I'd climb more mountains; I'd swim more rivers; I'd go more places I'd never been to; I'd eat more ice cream and fewer beans.

I'd have more actual troubles and fewer imaginary ones.

You see, I was one of those people who lived prophylactically and sensibly and sanely, hour after hour and day after day. Oh, I've had my moments, and if I had to do it over again, I'd have more of those moments—moment by moment by moment.

I've been one of those people who never went anywhere without a thermometer, a hot water bottle, a gargle, a raincoat, and a parachute. If I had to do it all over again, I'd travel lighter next time.

If I had it to do over again, I'd start barefoot earlier in the spring and stay way later in the fall. I'd ride more merry-go-rounds, I'd watch more sunrises, and I'd play with more children, if I had my life to live over again.

But you see, I don't.

And to this I would add, that even if we have lived our lives unwisely, and maybe even too seriously to this point, the Lord forgives and the Lord allows us to review and renew the style of our daily life in Him. The joy that we have in the Lord is a joy that has no bounds. That means that we don't need to *try* to be more joyful and get too serious about being joyful! It means, instead, that the Lord has given us His Spirit to empower and enable us to reach out to others in the joy that is ours, and always will be ours in the Lord Jesus!

Reflections

1. Write a 25-word summary of your life up to this point. Share it with a good friend.
2. Ask your family, your co-workers, and other friends to do the same. Share these reflections with each other.

LIGHTEN UP!

Don't tell me to have a good day! I felt like shouting one time when a friend offered this advice to me. If I want a crummy day, I'll have a crummy day.

He meant well. But I just wasn't in the mood for someone to insist that I have a good day. What did he care anyway?

In reflecting on that day, I think I was undergoing what many would label stress. Everything was wrong, nothing was right; and if everything hadn't gone wrong yet, just give it some time and it would. Do you have those kinds of days too?

I know my problem. I need to lighten up a bit. I need to step back and ask, are those things I'm getting upset about really all that important? One helpful test is to ask yourself, when getting uptight and tense, will this current situation make any difference to me or anyone else in the future?

Really, how important will it be next week that I was hung up in traffic tonight? Or that I forgot to buy everything I needed at the grocery store? Or that she is late again tonight? Or that the kids spilled their juice? And on and on and on.

I know that joy relieves stress. I know that I get too uptight about people not being on time. Now all I need to do is quietly step back and see that these uptight situations really aren't all that important.

Perhaps I should be getting more uptight about the hungry people in Africa, or the hurting family next door, or my friend who needs someone just to talk to.

"Lighten up" are good words to hear, as we hear them in love from our support people. We also hear the Lord's words, "Don't be afraid," and "don't worry," as He tells us that He is still in control. And then we can connect the I-am-the-light-of-the-world image to this lighten-up concept and see that they really do work hand in hand.

As we lighten up our lives and point to the Lord, we become lights to others to illuminate our Lord for them. A story about a boy who had a major part in a Sunday school program fits here nicely. He was memorizing his lines, a lot of them from the Scriptures. During the program, his mom sat in the front row in order to help him out in case he forgot his words. He was doing fine until he suddenly stopped, turned red, and looked at his mom for a cue. She whispered, but he couldn't remember. She gestured, but still he was lost. Finally, she cupped her hands and shouted, "I am the light of the world."

Of course, he thought. I should have remembered that. And he quickly calmed down and continued by shouting, "My mother is the light of the world!"

And he was right. She was a light to him and to the world. And that boy, also, is a light of the world, just like we all are lights of the world, as we lighten up and point others to the true Light, Jesus Christ!

Reflections

1. In what areas of your life do you need to lighten up?

2. How can you help someone close to you lighten up?

HOW TO KEEP HAPPY AND HEALTHY

Here are 12 suggestions for you to consider as God helps keep you happy and healthy. They will help to develop a positive mind-set, and will also help you to focus on the priorities in life.

1. Think out loud. One thing I wish I would have done more of when my kids were younger was to think out loud to them. I kept too many of my thoughts and worries to myself. It would have been more helpful to me, and to them, if I would have been more open about my concerns, doubts, and joys. I would have modeled for them the importance of honest sharing and openness with those around you.

2. Ask "what if" questions. Dream dreams and see visions by asking the big question, *What if?* It helps you re-think your priorities and open up your mind to new and creative ideas. The companion question is *Why not?* rather than *Why?* This type of questioning will help you see situations in new ways.

3. Look at one thing and see something else. That's a good definition of "creativity." It helps to keep your thoughts and mind open to new possibilities. For example, see a wait in traffic as a great time to pray or read or make some phone calls. Or look at all the symbols and items around you that remind you of your faith and the presence of the Lord. The water fountain is a sign of your Baptism, a loaf of bread reminds you of the Eucharistic meal. Street lights recall our calling as lights to the world. Let your mind do the connecting. It's fun, and it sure helps time fly!

4. Look for other ways of doing things. Drive to the office on a different route tomorrow. Have lunch at a new place next week. Fix breakfast for your spouse as a surprise next Saturday. Get up 30 minutes earlier tomorrow and take a hike around the block. The idea is to break out of any kind of "schedule slump" in which you might find yourself. Try it; it's fun!

5. Avoid falling in love with your own ideas. That's not easy to do. They're so good, right? Maybe so, but there are always other ways of doing things. Listen to others' suggestions. See how your own thoughts can be improved. And try to understand that there is more than one way to do most anything!

6. Be an "inverse paranoid." An inverse paranoid is someone who thinks everyone is out to make him happy! Try it. It works. Just imagine everyone you meet is trying to bring happiness and joy to your life. And then try to do the same for them. It is a marvelous way to relate to people!

7. *Be a pro-active risk-taker.* Because Christ has already done everything that needs to be done for our eternal life, we are able to risk our time, our resources, ourselves to reach out to other people. We can risk being uncomfortable. We can risk being taken advantage of. We can risk negative reactions from others because the Lord is on our side. A friend of mine says that whenever someone feels down or depressed, there are 10 things they should do: First, they should reach out to help someone in need, and then they should repeat that action 9 more times!

8. *Lighten up—we have the last word!* And whenever we get discouraged, we can remind each other of the promise of the Lord: "I will be with you always, to the end of the age" (Matt. 28:20). That gives us the last laugh. Joy and humor and celebration are ours because Christ had the last laugh on the devil. The Friday before Easter is called Good because of Christ's victory that followed on the first Easter morning! And that means that for every Good Friday in our lives, there's always an Easter.

9. *Ask others for help.* How helpfully freeing it is to be able to ask others for assistance. It shows that we do not have everything together in our own lives, it affirms those who ask for help, and it points out that all of us need others for guidance and direction. Think of how you feel when someone asks you for help. Especially if you

have something to offer, you feel quite good about it. Seeking help is not a sign of weakness, but rather it is a sign of strength. We need other people in order to fulfill life's purpose. Go ahead and ask!

10. *Be a divine irritant.* I like that phrase. It sounds like fun. It sounds like we need those kind of people around us as much as possible. For it is they who nudge and push us and help us to look at and answer some of the tougher questions in life. These are the people who sometimes can get to you, but they do their irritating in such a way, that somehow you know they are speaking prophetically, and that they really are attempting to help you do a better job and be a better person. So risk raising those tough questions. Push those around you to look clearly at what they are doing in their lives. Seek to share a word of love and hope while helping a friend be aware of the total implications of his actions and activities.

11. *Keep focused on the cross and the empty tomb.* This says to me that worship and personal Bible study are "givens" to God's people. Anything that helps get us back on track, anything that allows us to evaluate our priorities is essential in living a joy-filled life.

And what a better way to do this than to gather around the Scriptures as God's people to affirm, support, and befriend one another as the Lord builds us up in the faith!

12. *Live joyfully in the forgiveness that is yours each day!* What a powerful gift we have

from the Lord! It's forgiveness. A way to begin each day new and renewed. A way of seeing life through the cross and empty tomb which shows us how to forgive others as God continues to forgive us. A powerful testimony to the Lord at work in our lives. Can you imagine what life would be like if there were no forgiveness? As one pastor said, "It would be hell!" And he meant it quite literally! All of our joy and hope and celebrations are grounded in the fact that God has forgiven us in Christ Jesus, and that we are now able to love and forgive others. Where does our joy come from? From God, who forgives!

These 12 suggestions are not sure-fire how-tos at being happy and healthy, but they can be helpful suggestions as we continue to share our faith and love in the Lord, and provide comfort and support to those around us. And in so doing, it is exciting to see that we'll be serving the Lord while we're at it!

Reflections

1. Which of the 12 suggestions above is most helpful to you?
2. Think of other suggestions you would add to this list, and share them with a friend.

THE MAIN THING

The main thing is to keep the main thing the main thing.

I like this statement. Whether it was said by Martin Luther, George Washington, or Grandma Schultz, it is still worth repeating again and again.

We keep a healthy perspective on life when we do keep the main thing the main thing. It is when we stray from God's focus for our lives that we become unhealthy and stressed out.

The main thing, of course, is Jesus Christ. But many people do not realize this. And even when they do, it is easy to let priorities go awry. To remember that Jesus is the main thing in our lives does not mean that we spend 20 hours a day at church, reading the Bible. It does mean that we continue to ask our Lord for help in keeping Him as the focus of our lives. And the Good News is that even when we fail to do this, the Lord forgives us and woos us back to His fold.

What competes with Jesus as the main thing in your life? Self, spouse, work, kids, home, sports, studying, accomplishments? All of the above? All of these are certainly important and all of them can be blessings and gifts of the Lord. The key is seeing them as just that—gifts to us—to use, share, love, and affirm!

Aunt Caroline died years ago, and her family laid a white Bible in her coffin. When asked why it was there, her family said that the Bible was such an important part of her life, that it just seemed appropriate to keep it with her. That picture of Aunt Caroline and the Bible got me to thinking—what would people want to put in my casket as a reminder of what was important to me in life? Maybe a TV knob, or a beer can top, or a newspaper, or a football, or a road map, or an office key, or . . . ?

What would people think of putting into your casket?

Reflections

1. Discuss the question above with family and friends.

2. How can others see Christ as the main thing in your life?

A PERSONAL MISSION STATEMENT

"For to me, to live is Christ and to die is gain" (Phil. 1:21, NIV)—not a bad statement of purpose, from our friend St. Paul.

Here's an exercise for you to do. Try writing out a 25-word statement of your purpose for living. Try to be personal, specific, honest, and realistic. What is important to you in life? What are you trying to accomplish? What would you like people to remember you for after you are gone? What would you like written on your tombstone?

Below is some space to write a statement. You may want to test out some of what we have been discussing in this book, to see if it works. After you are finished, ask other friends and family to do the same and then compare mission statements.

It is helpful to review your statement every few weeks and compare what your statement says with how you are spending your hours and what your priorities seem to be.

Ideally they would be to

- celebrate life as a gift of God, and

- joyfully help others do the same by caring and relating to people through forgiveness in Christ.

Reflections

1. In the space below, write out your own personal mission statement.

My Mission Statement

2. Share your statement with someone else and ask others to share their statements with you.

BENEFITS OF HUMOR

We like to be around happy people, right? I sure do. Never yet have I heard a survey point out that most people like to hang around dull and boring people. Studies point out that young people and adults enjoy people who are positive, happy, up-beat. This is not to say that we all like the joke-teller or the wise-guy. Humor is not telling jokes, but rather it is being sensitive to the human needs and realities of life.

Here are some of the benefits of encouraging humor in your home, your office, your congregation, your neighborhood:

1. Humor glorifies the Lord. It points people to the gift-giver. It says "Lord, here we are—take us and use us."

2. Humor keeps us human. It continually points out our flaws and mistakes. That's what's so great about humor. It allows us to laugh at ourselves. It forces us to not take ourselves too seriously! Some of the more popular comedians are those who point out their own frailties, who look at themselves and don't always like what they see. Louie Anderson, a hefty, over-sized comedian, often joked that he could never lie on the beach because people would always try to toss him back into the water!

3. Humor makes us rely on forgiveness. Humor, in pointing out our humanness, points out our sin. Humor can then be instrumental in showing how terribly hopeless we all are, except for the forgiveness we have in Christ Jesus!

4. Humor forces us to relate to others. Good, appropriate humor is people-focused. It helps bring people closer to each other. The shortest distance between two people is a smile. Or a gumball.

5. Humor relieves tension. A laugh, a chuckle, can do much to help people better relate to each other. Look for opportunities to break the ice when things get too serious. I remember being in a heated discussion about the requirements for being a professional church worker. It was a serious subject, but we were taking ourselves *too* seriously. Then someone suggested that there are really only two requirements for a church worker:
1. Gray hair to give a distinguished look.
2. Hemorrhoids to give a sorrowful look.

6. Humor commands attention. Ask a person what he or she remembers about a recent sermon. Often it is the human-interest or humorous story that was shared. Notice how effective speakers blend humorous anecdotes and serious content in their presentations. Humor does keep us listening. An effective speaker recently quoted J. Paul Getty on how to be successful. Getty said, "Rise early, work hard, and strike oil!" I do not remember too many other thoughts shared, but I do remember that one!

7. Humor removes barriers. It breaks down communication problems. It allows people to become less defensive and more at ease. A family was gathered around the death bed of a loved one. They were waiting for the end. One person remarked that he had read recently that people die only when their feet are cold. He further stated that no one was known to have died with warm feet. Just then the bed-ridden patient opened his eyes and said, "Joan of Arc did!" Barriers around the room that night were lifted!

8. Humor is an affirmation of others. To be able to laugh and joke with someone is indeed a compliment. It shows that two people, or more, have learned not to take themselves too seriously. It shows that they respect each other and can tell humorous stories and not be offended or put down. Humor says to people, I like and respect you so much that I can be honest and open with you!

9. Humor is a means of proclaiming the Good News of Jesus Christ! Yes, humor is an excellent way to confess and profess our faith. What a world this would be if more people could see that our Lord is a loving and happy God—One who had to have a sense of humor to have created the likes of us! Humor allows us to get beyond ourselves and our sins and share the faith we have in Jesus Christ. A little girl had the role of the Christmas angel one special Christmas Eve. She had memorized her lines well, but as she pranced out onto the stage with her silver wings flapping, she looked into the audience and saw her mom, grandpa, and all her friends. And she quickly for-

got her words! But, she was a good Christian, for even though she forgot the lines that went, "Fear not, for I have glad tidings of great joy," she did remember the meaning and quickly got herself back together and shouted out, "Boy, do I have good news for you!"

10. Humor is fun—it keeps us positive! A popular song once noted that the world needs "love, sweet love," but it also could use some hefty doses of humor! Humor is contagious—let's pray for an epidemic! Too many of us still go around as if Easter had not happened! But it has! And we are living on the "other side" of the Resurrection! That makes us "resurrection resources!"

Garrison Keillor once remarked that, for midwestern Lutherans, every day is Lent! What a horrible way to go through life. But look around us. Where is the resurrection? Where are the balloons and shouts of hooray and hugs of hope? Oh, they are there all right, the Lord is still in control. But there is so much more that we can do to bring more joy and hope and comfort to a world so in need of a happy and affirming Lord.

In a parish in Kansas City many years ago, a number of teenagers got the idea of sitting near the front and on the aisles in church. As members returned from communing, these young people intentionally caught each person's eye and shared a big smile with them. And it was contagious— to some people anyway. Some adults quickly looked away. Some weren't sure what to do. And others thought it certainly was disrespectful. But these young people felt different. They saw the Eucharist as a meal of thanksgiving and joy and hope!

But we also need to know that a number of adult leaders in that parish did not appreciate what those young people did. And their minister of youth and education certainly heard about it. And, by the way, you should also note that I am no longer serving that congregation!

Reflections

1. Review the benefits of humor. Which ones make the most sense to you?

2. Add some other benefits of humor. Attempt to put at least one of these in practice each week.

ADDING HUMOR TO YOUR LIFE

These ideas are adapted from *The Joyful Noiseletter*, the Fellowship of Merry Christians.

1. Hang out with people who make you laugh. Identify a funny friend, someone who always has something funny to say. Whom did you think of as you read this first suggestion? Spend time with this person on a regular basis.

2. Make a daily laughter appointment. Set a time each day when you are likely to be amused. Maybe it will be in front of the TV watching your favorite sitcom reruns. Maybe it will be reading

the comics in the daily paper. Maybe it will be with a group of friends at lunch. Set yourself up for a laugh every day.

3. Start a humor file. Pay attention to humorous events around you. Clip funny comics, misprints, and stories from the newspaper and magazines. Stick favorite cartoons on your mirror, the refrigerator, or inside your locker door. Write down the funny happenings of the day in your diary or journal. Go through your humor file whenever your spirit needs a lift.

4. Give the gift of laughter. Send funny cards to friends and relatives. Do the unexpected. Take a paperback collection of a favorite comic strip to a friend in the hospital.

5. Tell humorous true stories instead of jokes. You don't have to be a comedian to share the gift of humor. Personal stories that invite your friends to laugh with you are more natural, and less likely to flop, than carefully memorized jokes and well-timed punch lines.

6. Avoid and discourage humor that belittles, ridicules, or stereotypes any person or group. Humor is meant to heal, encourage, and sometimes to reveal a painful truth in a lighthearted manner. When humor hurts, it loses its holiness.

7. Laugh when you need to the most. In times of great sorrow, stress, or disappointment, laughter can be a welcome release of tension or nervous energy. There are times when laughter may seem inappropriate; but more often than not, a good laugh comes just before or just after a good cry.

8. Practice the art of laughter. Like many other worthwhile things, laughter is a learned and practiced skill. The more you do it, the better you will be at it. The less you laugh, the quicker you will lose the skill. Use it or lose it.

9. Look up the word joy *in a concordance or Bible dictionary.* Read the verses that talk about joy. Don't forget that Ecclesiastes reminds us there is a time for joy.

10. Think about the incarnational (God in the flesh) nature of laughter. Let the reality of God laughing with you and through you, as you experience happiness and fun in the world, sink into your heart!

Reflections

1. Decide to follow through on 2 or 3 of the suggested ideas above.

2. Share this list with a friend, and work together on adding new ideas to the list.

TIPS FOR EFFECTIVE HUMORISTS

So you say you want to be effective as a speaker and a humorist? These quick suggestions will not land you a spot on the Tonight Show, but they may be helpful in focusing your gift of humor.

Give them a look.

1. Know your audience. Obvious, but certainly very important. Try to understand their history, their stories, their purpose as individuals, a group, or organization; and then make your presentation connect with their hopes and plans.

2. Realize that some people are humor-insulated. There is a time and a place for everything, and sometimes a group is just not ready to enjoy each other, or even the speaker! I remember one time when I was speaking to a group (that will remain nameless), I was worried from the start because they really did not seem to be enjoying themselves, even during the meal. The MC finally came up to me and, breaking the dead silence in the room, said, "Are you ready to speak, or should we let them enjoy themselves for a while?"

3. Be natural. Don't force yourself. Be who you are—the Lord knew what He was doing when He made you! Do not try to be a great joke teller or story maker if those aren't your gifts. Instead, do what you do well—and give it all you've got! Whether in a meeting, at home around friends, or speaking at a banquet, continue to use the skills and gifts that are yours. You'll do better, feel better, and you'll be your natural humorous self!

4. Let humor aid communication without calling attention to itself. Humor is a means to an end. It can attract, entice, focus, but it should not become the main thing. Humor and humorous stories can get in the way of the message or the person. Check out the purpose and role of humor.

I have a little children's message which I have done a number of times which I always thought was effective, humorous, and certainly appropriate. I juggle three balls and tell the story of creation, and how God sent Jesus to put the world and people back together again. Kids seemed to like it, and I thought it was effective, for the most part. Until one day I heard some kids who had just heard this message talking to their parents.

"What did you learn at church this morning?" the parents asked.

"Oh, it was great," they replied. "This guy could juggle three balls. I hope I can juggle some day!" Here endeth the lesson!

5. Don't be offensive. Humor sometimes gets a bum rap because it can be misused. Humor is not being used appropriately when it becomes offensive to others. Never use stories or illustrations that might offend people.

6. Do not overdo it. A little humor goes a long way. Do not overkill. Give time to others to share and talk. A rule of thumb for speakers is "Be relevant, be humorous, be seated."

7. Affirm people through humor. Humor is a great way to support and give credit to people. Keep looking for ways to say helpful and affirming things to those around you.

8. Use yourself as a target for humor. If we can't laugh at ourselves, we're all in trouble. Poking fun at yourself helps to keep you human, and shows that you do not take yourself too seriously.

I enjoy telling stories about my family. That's because I enjoy my family, and to poke fun at them is like poking fun at myself. Our annual Christmas letter attempts to take lightly the yearly activities of our bunch. We became tired of hearing all of the "successes" of everyone else's family, so we decided 31 years ago to have fun picking and poking at each other through our Yuletide greeting. Our mothers still don't know what is true and what isn't, but it does keep them guessing! Last year we mentioned that our daughter-in-law, Jill, has roots in Iowa. As a matter of fact, she was the 1st runner-up in a recent Miss Iowa contest. She would have won, but during the talent contest, she couldn't get her tractor started!

9. Let others tell their stories. An effective humorist helps others to tell their stories too. I'm amazed at the number of people who come up to me after a presentation and tell their own story (or three). It must be because they have a need to tell someone their real stories, or else my stories are so bad that they are attempting to give me new material!

10. See everyone as having a sense of humor. That's because it's true. Assume they have the gift and you'll be surprised at the difference you see in them. Watch and listen for their hot button, what they like to talk about. And if they're grandparents, certainly ask them to see pictures of their grandchildren!

Reflections

1. Grade yourself or another speaker/presenter using these tips.

2. Evaluate a sermon on the basis of these ingredients. Note how humor was, or could have been, used to emphasize the biblical truths and application of the message.

NEGATIVE HUMOR

Humor, just like any other gift, can be misused. That may be one reason why humor and laughter are sometimes seen as being more "of the devil" than of the Lord.

Negative humor:

1. Pokes fun at others. It *laughs at*, rather than with, others.

2. Reflects *anger*.

3. *Offends* with inappropriate references to sex or profanity.

4. Divides a group with *put-downs*.

5. Uses *stereotypes*.

6. Presents stories that are *cruel, abusive, and offensive*.

7. Is *insensitive* to what causes pain in others.

8. *Negates* self-confidence.

9. Gives license to *hurt* someone.

10. *Infirms* rather than affirms people.

Reflections

1. Take note of a TV comedian in the coming days and measure his style of humor.

2. Be sensitive to your own stories and jokes, both those you tell and those which others tell you.

POSITIVE HUMOR

In contrast to stress-producing humor, stress-reducing humor is a positive and highly valuable gift of God. You can find much stress-reducing humor throughout the Scriptures as the Lord and His people relate to others with joy and forgiveness. John 15:11 captures this type of humor and much more: "I have told you this so that My joy may be in you and that your joy may be complete."

Positive humor:

1. Jokes about *human faults*.
2. Encourages people to *relax and relate*.
3. Pokes fun *at oneself*.
4. Builds *rapport* between people.
5. Creates a *supportive* atmosphere of fun and caring.
6. Notes positive aspects of *human relationships*.
7. Gives everyone a chance to *participate*.

Reflections

1. List other stress-reducing traits of positive humor.

2. Observe a speaker/preacher in action. Note the way positive humor is used.

TOO SERIOUS?
WHO, ME?

Yes, we all do take ourselves too seriously from time to time. It's human to do it. We very often try to run the universe, or at least our own little part of it. And the Lord must continue to smile at our foolishness, chuckle a little, let us do our thing, and then somehow get us back to realizing that He is the one in control after all.

Some of us go so far as to become "terminal professionals" where stress is the emblem of courage. We wallow all too much in our own busyness. We build our kingdoms, protect our turf, and spend hours worrying about what should have and could have happened. And the Lord smiles sadly, and maybe even cries a bit, and then woos us back to Himself.

We get into trouble by thinking that we always have to succeed. We know we are called, not to be successful, but to be faithful, but we continue to live by success-oriented goals. It's amazing to me that even the greatest baseball players, who hit .300 each year, are failing in their profession 70 percent of the time!

We also tend to think too highly of ourselves. We've worked hard, studied diligently, been led by God into our chosen profession, and all of this can and should be taken seriously. We get ourselves into trouble, however, when our position, or accomplishments, or schooling become more important than the message God calls us to proclaim. And to all this, the Lord says, "I have redeemed you, you are mine!"

We also compare ourselves with others and often come up on the short end of the continuum. Rather than rejoicing with those who rejoice we sometimes become jealous and envious of that better manager, the more effective communicator, the larger company, or the happier family.

We are also unable to accept our own limitations. Like the fabled animals who tried to be just like each other and thus lost their own individual gifts, we too can lose our gifts because we're jealous of others.

And finally, we take ourselves too seriously when we do not take our Lord seriously enough! When our energies move from the cross and empty tomb to our own worth and accomplishments, we certainly have a lifestyle that will wear us down and not focus on what the Lord has already done for us.

But rejoice! The Lord lives. And He forgives! And He has taken our own seriousness to the cross and exchanged it for a crown of life for us!

Reflections

1. When and why do you get too serious about yourself, your life?

2. What are some steps that can be helpful to you in breaking out of this seriousness into the light-heartedness of the Gospel?

NOT TAKING YOURSELF TOO SERIOUSLY

Here you have it, folks. Some guaranteed, successful, complete ways of turning your life into joy and celebration! (And if you believe all of this, you really are too serious!)

Take the following thoughts as they are, and as they are intended to be—words for you to meditate upon, write down, use, and at least consider putting to practice in your daily life. And add some of your own. And share them with others!

1. Know that you are loved, in Christ Jesus— now, forever!

2. Take God seriously—but don't take yourself too seriously!

3. God accepts us as we are—with our gifts and limitations. He asks us to do the same.

4. It is not helpful to accept our present mood as permanent. Moods and attitudes change. When we are down and depressed, we have the

assurance from the Lord that this too shall pass. When we are up and on top of things, we rejoice, but know that this will not last forever. Be helpful to others around you, as you perceive their moods and needs.

5. *Surround yourself with positive support people.* Help each other.

6. *Continue to affirm your worthiness in Christ.*

7. *See Christ in the people around you.* He is and He is here—the signs are all around us!

8. *Stop trying to prove yourself.* Allow the Lord to work through you to reach others in joy and humility.

9. *God's mercies are new each day—regardless of how you look, feel, or act.*

10. *Try getting up differently each morning.* Do new things. Think new thoughts.

11. *Look for uniqueness and diversity in others.* Find out and celebrate your differences with others.

12. *See life, and aging, as a gift and not a disease.*

13. *Have a good laugh at yourself, at least once a day—and twice on Sundays!* Laughter is a way of crossing ourselves!

14. *Care for people; don't try to cure them.*

15. *Sing a lot!* Do it publicly or privately, depending on your gifts! That's a great way of rejoicing in the Lord! And it helps those around you to wonder what you are up to in your life!

16. Affirm people, instead of infirming them. Free others up to celebrate the presence of the Lord.

17. Make a joy list. Each day write out events and activities that help you celebrate and share your joy in the Lord. Add to it each day. It's a great way to live out your life as a celebrating saint!

18. Make a happy journal. Write about people and events that bring happiness to you. Include these people in your prayers. Pray also for those who bring grief and despair to you. Perhaps you can someday put them on your happy list!

19. See our strength in the Word and Sacraments. And remember your Baptism—daily!

20. Summary of the above—FORGIVE-NESS! Even when we do take ourselves too seriously!

Reflections

1. Add to this list some of your favorite ways to keep positive and celebrative.
2. Attempt to live out these 20 suggestions, plus your own, one day at a time. Make a prayer list and add people to it daily, praying for their joy in the Lord.

LAUGHING MATTERS

These pages continue to emphasize the importance of taking our Lord very seriously and ourselves lightly. That is why, or so it is said, that angels can fly! Sounds good to me!

Let's look at other ways to make the point that laughing really does matter. It is a gift from God that has great potential for turning the church and the world around. Here are 15 more suggestions for pointing out that laughing does indeed matter.

1. Life is too serious to be taken seriously.

2. The resurrection is the focus of our joy and celebration.

3. Laugh at yourself first, before anyone else can.

4. Laughter is the shortest distance between two people.

5. You do not have to teach people to be funny—you only have to give them permission.

6. It is more important to have fun than to be funny.

7. Give "ah-ha's" through "ha-ha's." Meaningful and significant learning can be gained through effective use of humor.

8. For something to be funny, it has to "smell" real.

9. Nothing is funnier than the unintended humor of reality.

10. Life is what happens when you have something else planned. God invented time so that everything doesn't happen all at once!

11. Take a piece of reality, hold it to a mirror, and twist it a little—that's humor.

12. Laughter is God's hand on the shoulder of a troubled world.

13. Holy laughter is a gift of grace. It is the human spirit's last defense against sin and despair.

14. We can laugh because we know how it all turns out in the end—Christ is victorious!

15. Laughter is a blunt, brilliant, brave affirmation that death is not the final answer. Holy mirth is keeping sight of Christ's final victory over death.

Reflections

1. Which of the above makes the most sense to you? How can you apply it to your daily life?
2. Think of a number of persons to whom to send a postcard, sharing one of these statements. Not only will you make the post office happy, you'll make your friends happy also!

AT OR *WITH?*

An issue of the newsletter *Laughing Matters* differentiates between laughing with and at others.

Laughing with others . . .

- is based on caring and empathy.
- builds confidence and is supportive.
- involves everyone in the fun.

- allows the initiator to be the butt of the joke.
- pokes fun at universal human foibles.
- goes for the *jocular* vein.

Laughing at others . . .

- is based on contempt and insensitivity.
- destroys confidence.
- excludes and offends some people.
- divides people.
- reinforces stereotypes by singling out a particular group as the "butt of the joke."
- goes for the jugular vein.

Reprinted with permission from *Laughing Matters* magazine, edited by Joel Goodman and published by The HUMOR Project, Inc., 110 Spring St., Saratoga Springs, NY 12866.

Reflections

1. List other thoughts under "Laughing with others" from experiences in your own life.

2. List other thoughts under "Laughing at others" from experiences in your own life.

WORM THEOLOGY

I remember singing a phrase in a hymn, "For such a worm as I," as a little kid. It didn't make that much of an impression on me then, but it is indicative of the sense that we all are poor, worthless worms, and who wants to be one of them?

Worm Theology emphasizes our own sinfulness, instead of the forgiveness and redemption that is ours in Christ Jesus. Sinful, worthless worms—oh yes. But forgiven worms, that's better yet!

Perhaps the problem for some of us is that we have grown up thinking that the emphasis is on us worms, rather than on the joy of knowing that Christ has redeemed and saved us.

This is not to suggest that we ignore and downplay our sinful connection. Just the opposite. We confess our sinfulness and move to the cross for our redemption, and the assurance of what Christ has done for us. The cross of Christ is what makes us right. Nothing that we do on our own, not even our celebrating, is appropriate, if Christ is not the central focus of our joy and celebration.

Reflections

1. Recall your feelings as a young child, sitting in church. Did you feel like a worm, or a sinner forgiven by Christ?

2. Ask other people in your family and church their views of their growing up years in church. What positive and negative feelings do they remember?

AND GOD CREATED LAUGHTER

In discussing the gift of laughter and its relationship to the fall, Conrad Hyers in his book,

And God Created Laughter, writes:

"The fall is, if anything, the loss of laughter, not the loss of seriousness. Adam and Eve fell when they began to take themselves, their deprivations, and ambitions too seriously. And we have taken ourselves, our opinions and beliefs, our status and achievements, and our designs on the universe too seriously ever since."

Hyers looks at the Bible as divine comedy with God as the divine humorist. The comedy he speaks of is not to be associated with modern day humor: nor is it an attempt to demean or make fun of the Scriptures. The biblical comedy which Hyers "pulls right out of the text" ranges from the experiences of Jonah to those who are not ashamed of the Gospel and are tools for Christ. It is Christ alone, through the foolishness of the Gospel, who not only breaks us down so He can use us, but who in the process makes beautiful what was once ugly and hideous.

Hyers continues, "Jesus freely used humor, irony, and satire to that end. His descriptions of the hypocrisies of the Pharisees use overtly humorous images: the blind leading the blind; straining out a gnat, then swallowing a camel; meticulously cleaning the outside of a cup while leaving the inside filthy . . ."

From *And God Created Laughter: The Bible As Divine Comedy*, Conrad Hyers. Louisville: Westminster John Knox Press, 1987. Used by permission.

Reflections

1. Look through the Scriptures to pick out stories that show God's sense of humor. Share these

with others.

2. How do you rate your congregation in terms
   of its celebrative spirit and style? Look at various aspects of the congregation and do a study
   of the joy and seriousness that are both
   needed.

LIFE IS FOR GIVING

Each day is a new day for you and for me. We
begin each morning refreshed from a good nights
sleep (hopefully!) and, more than that, knowing
that the Lord has forgiven us and given us a new
day as a gift. Isaiah 43:18–19 says it well, "Do not
cling to events of the past or dwell on what happened long ago. Watch for the new thing I am
going to do. It is happening already—you can see
it now!"

Our own mindset towards life, the reason for
being able to take each day as a new start, is due
to God's love and forgiveness. It is this fact that
provides us with a healthy attitude of being able
to laugh at life, live in the power of His forgiveness, and be able to start each new day with a
clean slate. So what if we messed yesterday up.
Okay, so we acted foolishly. Yes, yes we know
that it was a dumb thing to say—that's all history
now, and this Lord provides us with a fresh new
day.

So go on out today and try your wings. Go fly high in the Lord, knowing that God has given you an excellent flight plan. No sense clinging to yesterday, because today has so much in store for you!

Reflections

1. Reflect on some past occurrences that you can let go of today.
2. What new thing are you going to watch for today from the Lord?

FEELING GOOD ABOUT YOURSELF

A 55-year-old recently said to me, "According to the U.S. Census Bureau, the average American is 33-years-old. Well, at least I'm above average at something!"

Where do you get your sense of worth in life? Many people feel worthwhile through their own accomplishments. Some do it through their position of power and authority. Others feel good only in comparison to how poorly others perform.

As we live and focus our life in the Lord, He allows us to see that our worth is really all tied up in what Christ has already done for us. God calls all of us winners. All of us are above average. All of us have made the grade because of what Christ has done in dying and rising for us.

Feeling down and rejected? Look at the cross and empty tomb! Failed again? Read the Scriptures to see how God loves you! Ready to give up? See the love and comfort of God's people around you!

And when we meet others who feel down and rejected, we are able to become a voice of hope, a message of love, and a sign of God's presence among them also.

Reflections

1. Name a person whom you think is feeling down and depressed. What can you do for that person today?

2. What are some ways that you use for sensing and knowing God's love for you each day?

DEFINING HUMOR

What is humor anyway? Why is it so important to us? How come the Lord gave it to us as a gift?

These questions may indeed be helpful and intriguing, but let's not go overboard on attempting to diagnose this gift. Rather, let's plan on using and developing this gift more in ourselves and in other people. It was Robert Benchley who said, "Defining and analyzing humor is a pastime of humorless people."

Or another way to make the point is to suggest that trying to define humor is like trying to dissect a frog. In the process you learn something about the anatomy of the frog—but it sure ruins the frog!

Another humorous type defined humor as the mind sneezing. Think about that one for a while! Will Rogers once said that everything was funny as long as it was happening to someone else!

So, let's get on with using the gift of humor. Let it happen. Rejoice in being able to laugh and smile and keep life in perspective. And keep providing the opportunities for others to grab your style of humor, and theirs, and use it to proclaim the joy we have in the Lord!

Reflections

1. Write down humorous sayings you hear. Make a scrapbook and keep it handy for daily conversations.
2. How do you define humor? This is a good question to discuss with a friend.

HUMOR IN YOUR CONGREGATION

Books could be, and have been, written about the marvelous humor that continually happens in our congregations. Isn't it great that the Lord allows His community of people to laugh and smile and be human in the place called church!

Church, the communion of saints, the gathering of saints, your congregation is an exciting mixture of people of all ages and backgrounds. And the gift of humor continues to help effective parishes go about proclaiming and nurturing and reaching out to others with God's love and forgiveness in Christ.

It was said once by someone with an obviously good sense of humor that, "the reason mountain climbers are all tied together is to keep the sane ones from going home!" And that's a good picture of the congregation, as well. Here we are, a group of sinful, human, searching people, gathered together in order to focus on our Lord Jesus Christ. The world looks at us and wonders what we are all about. And we gather together, out of an insane world, to build one another up in the faith that is ours in Christ!

What is fun about your congregation? Or, if it isn't fun, what can you do to bring some celebration into these pews and pulpit? I recently saw a worship bulletin that listed "gossip" as the sermon topic. Right after the sermon, the next hymn to be sung was "I Love to Tell the Story!" Now I think that's funny! And I even think God is chuckling at that one.

Reflections

1. Think of a recent humorous incident in your congregation. Share it with a friend.

2. What barriers inhibit your congregation from sharing humor and happiness? How can these barriers be taken down?

THE HUMOR OF CHILDREN

If you want to see humor in its best form, watch and listen to kids. Listen as they hear words used in worship and around the home and share what their little minds do with adult concepts and theologies. I think when the Lord suggested that we old adults become like children, He was also suggesting that we recapture some of that child-like innocence and trust and fresh humor once again.

A Sunday school student was drawing a picture of God. His teacher said, "No one knows what God looks like."

The child replied, "Now they do!"

Two little 5-year-olds were listening to their teacher ask a question. "Now, students, what has a bushy tail, climbs trees, gathers nuts, and is furry?"

They thought a while and then one said softly to his friend, "It sounds like a squirrel, but I bet the answer is Jesus."

What does this tell us about how we look for the right answer in our classes and instructions?

Another little boy was asked to name one of the "sharpest" books of the Bible. The little wise guy said, "The Axe of the Apostles."

It is certainly refreshing to see and sense the humor of children. Too bad some people lose that zest for life, and sense of the beauty of laughter and innocence, as they grow older. Let's pray that all of us stay "young in the Lord" for all of our lives!

Reflections

1. Recall a humorous story or incident where children were involved.

2. Talk to youngsters about their joy in the Lord. See what you can learn from them.

DOWN WITH "GROAN-UPS"

I have nothing against old people. I am getting to be one of them myself.

But I am against grown-up people who have become "groan-ups," people who have lost the joy and celebration of life in the Lord. Now I'm sure they still love the Lord, and He still loves them, but wouldn't it be better if somehow they could break out of their serious adult mode and become "like a kid" again?

I heard of an 87-year-old who is a great example of a celebrating grown-up. Her family was placing her in a nursing home so she could get appropriate care and attention. Grandma was all for this and ready to be with her peers. As they entered her new home, she immediately spotted an old, quiet gentleman sitting all by himself in the corner. She shuffled over to her new-found friend, looked at him and said, "You remind me of my third husband!"

Taken aback, and not knowing what to say to this aggressive woman, the old man simply asked, "Well, how many husbands have you had?"

Whereby she promptly replied, "Two!" Now that's really celebrating life!

Let's begin a crusade to help us older folks sense and share the joy of the Lord. Older adults are often tremendous models for others to be able to share how the Lord has worked through their lives. Let's take advantage of these gifts that older persons possess! Wouldn't it be a better world? Wouldn't the Lord smile on us all as He sees young and old alike playing and laughing and hugging each other?

I say, Down with groan-ups! Up with smiles! Starting with me!

Reflections

1. Think of an over-65-year-old who is a great example of living joyfully in the faith. Tell that person how much you appreciate that example.

2. Think of a "groan-up" in your life. How can you be helpful in continuing to share the joy we have in the Lord with this person?

LOVE
NOTES

Aren't love notes great? These are the little messages that people leave in appropriate places throughout our lives. I see a sign on my pillow after Hazel leaves for a meeting that says, "Have a good day—I love you." You see a post-it on the refrigerator that reminds you, in love, that your supper is in the freezer. A little child writes on the blackboard before school, "Teacher, you're nice."

What a great way to share joy, God's love for others, and your care and concern. What a great way to help us keep healthy and happy! And sometimes love notes that are meant to be strong affirmations can turn out otherwise, and still keep us laughing.

Take the true story of Diane and Susie who many years ago went to their church building to say hi to their pastor. Fortunately for him, he was not in. But these two little 8-year-olds left a note under his office door. It read, "Dear Pastor, We like you. We think you are nice. We like your sermons. We just can't wait to understand them! Love, Diane and Susie."

Thanks, girls, for adding to our healthy attitude towards life! May God continue to encourage you to write many more love notes!

Reflections

1. Write a love note to someone special each week. It will do wonders for them—and you.
2. Read the greatest love note of them all, 1 Corinthians 13. Share it with someone else.

CHURCH BULLETINS REVISITED

Church bulletins can be a great place to look for humor. I sometimes think that the Lord sneaks those "mis-cues" in just to see if we are paying attention.

Some of my favorites are:

• The flowers on the altar will be given to those who are sick after the service.

• Join choir this week. Come to church on Thursday at 7:00 P.M. and sin.

• Our monthly Bible study will be held next Tuesday morning. It will be gin with breakfast at 6:30 A.M.

• Announcement: Thank You, Lord, for our preacher today. Fill him with good stuff and nudge him when he's said enough.

• The pastor, going on vacation, left this announcement: "I will be gone for the next two Sundays. The preacher during that time will be

pinned to the church bulletin board, and all births, marriages, and funerals will be postponed until my return."

Isn't it good to laugh at ourselves? We're not making fun of the church secretary or pastor, but we are thanking them for keeping us humble, and for helping us to recall some of the mistakes in our lives. Mistakes only force us that much more to focus on Christ, who has come to erase all of our mis-cues in life.

Reflections

1. Recall some of the bulletin bloopers you remember seeing.

2. How do you feel when you make a mistake that is obvious to many others? How does Christ's redeeming work help you in that situation?

3. How can you help others to accept their mistakes as signs of being human, and remind them of Christ's acceptance of each of us?

HUMOR IN HEAVEN

Of course heaven will be full of laughter and celebration. But let's not wait until then to get the party going!

Martin Luther once said, during an obvious fun evening of sharing, that if there is not humor in heaven, then "I don't want to go!"

What will you be celebrating in heaven? I want to spend time with my dad and get to know him better than I did here on earth. I imagine he was a real fun person, but I never got to experience him that way.

I'll also want to talk to the Lord about some of His humorous stunts like, why did He make an animal like the aardvark. Or why did He make broccoli? And why on earth is it that too many people seem to associate Him with somber seriousness instead of holy mirth?

Another good thing about God's plan for us is that we do not need to look forward to eternal life, because, in Christ, we are enjoying it right now!

And that's something to celebrate, even on this side of heaven!

Reflections

1. What are some questions you want to ask the Lord when you get to heaven?
2. With whom do you want to celebrate when you get to heaven?

FOR THE FUN OF IT

I'm convinced that the Lord created laughter just to hear and see His creation enjoy life. Sure, laughter is healthy for you; it reduces stress; it helps you relax. But I think it is okay to enjoy laughing just because it is fun to do, with no other purpose.

I often look for comical, off-the-wall stories, just to keep my laughing muscles in shape. Here is such a letter, that has little purpose, except to affirm the fun and joy of laughing.

Dear Son,

I'm writing this slow cause I know you can't read fast. We don't live in the same place we did when you left. Your dad read in the paper where most accidents happen within twenty miles from home, so we moved. I won't be able to send you the address because the last family that lived here took the numbers with them when they left, so they wouldn't have to change their address. This place has a washing machine. The first day I put four shirts in and pulled the chain and haven't seen them since. It only rained twice this week, three days the first time, and four days the second time.

Aunt Sue said the coat you wanted me to send you would be a little too heavy to send in the mail with those heavy buttons on it. So we cut them off and put them in the pocket.

About your father—he has a lovely new job. He has 500 men under him. He is cutting grass at the cemetery.

About your sister, she had a baby this morning, but I don't know if it's a boy or a girl, so I can't tell if you're an aunt or an uncle.

Uncle John fell in the whiskey vat. Some men tried to pull him out, but he fought them off manfully, and he drowned. We cremated him; he burned for three days.

Three of your friends went off the bridge in the pickup. One was driving, the other two were in the back. The driver got out. He rolled his window down and swam to safety. The other two drowned—they couldn't get the tailgate down.

Not much more news this time; nothing much has happened.

Love,
Mom

P.S. I was going to send you some money, but the envelope was already sealed.

Reflections

1. How do you react to this letter? What makes it funny, or not so funny to you?
2. Look and listen for other examples of stories that can make you laugh—just for the fun of it.

HAPPY
ARE
THEY

Our Lord shares an astonishing list in the Sermon on the Mount (Matt. 5:3–10). It is another way of stating that God's people's trust is to turn the world upside down as they share the Good News of what Jesus Christ has done for all people.

An educator has rephrased these words, not to change or belittle or add to the Scriptures, but rather, in a humorous way, to point out how we all misread or misinterpret the Scriptures from time to time in our own lives. Here is how his paraphrase goes:

Then Jesus took His disciples up the mountain and, gathering them around Him, He taught them saying:

"Blessed are the poor in spirit, for theirs is the kingdom of heaven.
Blessed are the weak.
Blessed are they that mourn,
Blessed are the merciful.
Blessed are they who thirst for justice.
Blessed are you when persecuted,
Blessed are you when you suffer.
Be glad and rejoice for your reward is great in heaven."

Then Simon Peter said, "Do we have to write this down?"

And Andrew said, "Are we supposed to know this?"

And James said, "I don't have any paper."

And Bartholomew said, "Do we have to turn this in?"

And John said, "The other disciples didn't have to learn this."

And Matthew said, "Can I go to the boys' room?"

And Judas said, "What does this have to do with real life?"

Then one of the Pharisees who was present asked to see Jesus' lesson plan and inquired of Jesus, "Where are your anticipatory set and your objectives in the cognitive?"

And Jesus wept.

Reflections

1. How do you react to this different look at Matthew 5?

2. What does it say to you about how we accept and react to God's Word?

FOR YOUTH ONLY

Here are a few suggestions to young people regarding how they can more effectively raise their parents. A big task, but with help like this, a fun task indeed.

1. Don't be afraid to speak your parents' language. Try to use strange-sounding phrases like,

"I'll help you with the dishes," or "I think I'll clean my room."

2. *Consider the TV shows your parents watch.* If you are concerned about their selection, try discussing the redeeming social values of Lawrence Welk with them.

3. *Try to understand their music.* Play Andy Williams' "Moon River" on the stereo until you are accustomed to the sound.

4. *Be patient with the underachiever.* When you catch your dieting mom sneaking salted peanuts, do not show your disapproval; tell her you like fat mothers.

5. *Encourage your parents to talk about their problems.* Try to keep in mind that, to them, things like earning a living and paying off the mortgage seem important.

6. *Be tolerant of their appearance.* When your dad gets a haircut, don't feel personally humiliated. Remember, it's important for him to look like his peers.

7. *If they do something you consider wrong, let them know it's their behavior you dislike, not them.*

8. *When they begin to talk about the Good Old Days, remind them gently that you do not remember the sinking of the Titanic and that Thomas Dewey is not your choice for president.*

9. *Suggest that your parents bring their friends home to meet you.* Let them know that "their friends are your friends" and "your home is their home." Also check to see if their friends

have any sons or daughters that might interest you.

10. Show your interest by asking your parents, "How did it go at work today? When they respond "okay" or "so-so," ask if they learned anything today! That should immediately end all conversation for the next hour!

A Must: Do share the love and forgiveness of Christ Jesus with them daily through I-love-you words and action hugs and allow them to do the same with you!

Reflections

1. What kind of relationship do you think parents and young people would have if they were to talk this way to each other?

2. Consider ways that you can be helpful in providing more opportunities for youth and adults to talk and be with each other in meaningful settings.

HUMOR IN OLD AGE

Old age is a gift. It is not a disease, as some people treat it. Unfortunately, old age is often stereotyped as something negative. We speak of the "young at heart," instead of the "old at heart." We make fun of our old bodies, much in jest, but often quite seriously.

There's a story about an older person who asked his doctor how his body compared to other men his age. The doctor asked, "Living or dead?"

For those of us who are quickly becoming older adults, we can help the situation by keeping our age in perspective. Okay, so our body can't do everything the mind tells it to do. So maybe our jogging pace has become equivalent to a galloping clam. Who cares? Life is still to be celebrated! I once heard a 17th century prayer spoken at a conference. It goes like this, and picks up the celebrative attitude that we old folks can continue to champion:

Lord, Thou knowest better than I know myself that I am growing older and will someday be old. Keep me from the fatal habit of thinking I must say something on every subject and on every occasion. Release me from craving to straighten out everyone's affairs. Make me thoughtful but not moody, helpful but not bossy. With my vast store of wisdom, it seems a pity not to use it all, but Thou knowest, Lord, that I want a few friends at the end.

Keep my mind free from the recital of endless details; give me wings to get to the point. Seal my lips on my aches and pains. They are increasing, and love of rehearsing them is becoming sweeter as the years go by. I dare not ask for grace enough to enjoy the talks of other's pains, but help me to endure them with patience.

I do not ask for an improved memory, but for a growing humility and a lessening cocksureness when my memory seems to clash with the memories of others. Teach me the glorious lesson that occasionally I may be mistaken.

Keep me reasonably sweet; I do not want to be a saint—some of them are so hard to live with— but a sour old person is one of the crowning works of the devil. Give me the ability to see good things in unexpected people. And give me, Lord, the grace to tell them so. Amen.

What an attitude! What a prayer!

Lord, grant all of us old folks the joy of aging and may we continue to be positive models of what it means to be saints, but saints that are easy to live with!

Reflections

1. Who are some of your favorite older persons? Why? Tell them so.
2. What can you do to help older persons enjoy life more to its fullest? Look for older persons around you who need a voice of hope and joy in their life.

BEING CHEERFUL

Proverbs 17:22 says it so well: "Being cheerful keeps you healthy. It is slow death to be gloomy all the time."

I ache for people who are not able to enjoy life and share their hope in the Lord with others. Perhaps the only thing we can do for them is to continue to share the "hope that is within us" in a loving and caring way. And we also need to be careful that we model that our joy is from the Lord, and not from any sense of being "more blessed" by the Lord than others.

A pastor once said, "When you speak of heaven, let your face light up and be irradiated with reflected glory. And when you speak of hell . . . well, then your everyday face will do." He was kidding, of course, but also trying to point out that we are called to be cheerful in the Lord!

Proverbs provides excellent medicine for God's people to stay healthy. Cheerfulness will not prohibit illness and accidents, but it will enable God's people to sense and see the presence of our joy-filled Lord in daily life.

Reflections

1. Look through the book of Proverbs and select other passages that deal with health and happiness.
2. Be sure to speak to someone today about the "hope that is within you."

PRAISE

Where compliments outnumber complaints, there is much joy and peace. Whether it is in our family, church, workplace, or neighborhood, we all need and look for praise and affirmation. When we hear good things about ourselves, when we praise our spouse and offspring, we and they tend to become like others believe we are. Praise and compliments will not make a person conceited. The opposite is true.

Doesn't it feel good when someone recognizes you and compliments you for a job well done? It's another one of those gifts from God that enables us and others to reach more closely our full potential.

The tragedy for many people is that they can go for days and days without hearing from others a word of hope and praise. And that is devastating. One worker said, "The only time my boss notices what I do is when I don't do it!"

So let's look for those people who need to hear about their worthiness in the Lord, and those who need to hear that they have gifts to share with others. Psalm 111 says it so well: "Praise the Lord! With all my heart I will thank the Lord in the assembly of His people . . . The Lord does not let us forget His wonderful actions . . . He is to be praised forever."

Praise the Lord! And praise others for their gifts as another way of praising the Lord and Creator of us all! And to this, all we can say again is, "Praise the Lord!"

Reflections

1. Who in your life needs to hear words of praise and affirmation?

Who better than you to share your faith with this person?

2. The psalms are excellent examples of praise and thanksgiving to the Lord of all. Plan to read all 150 of them in the coming weeks.

THE GIFT
OF LISTENING

God has given us two ears and one mouth so that we can listen twice as much as we speak!

Listening is such a gift. We thank the Lord for the listeners He has put around us—people who feel so good about themselves that they have the energy, not to tell, but simply to listen to others.

Here's an idea. Why not write out a 3″ × 5″ card that says,

The Gift of Listening

This certificate entitles you to one-half hour of my undivided attention. I will listen to you sincerely and carefully. I will not try to tell you anything, I will not interrupt, and I'll only ask questions if they would be helpful to you.

When would you like your gift?

Signed, The Listener

"Be still," the Lord tells us, "and know that I am God." Great advice as we listen to Him, in order to become better listeners to others.

Reflections

1. Think of one or two people in your life who need to be listened to. Do what you can to listen.

2. Perhaps you are one of those people. Ask a friend to allow you to share your thoughts, dreams, doubts.

HUMOR AND PROBLEMS GO TOGETHER

Gail Sheehy, in her book *Pathfinders* states that people who grow, succeed, and have a sense of well-being were found to practice four basic coping skills:

1. Work more.
2. Depend on friends.
3. Pray.
4. See humor in situations.

Sheehy adds, "Humor, like hope, allows one to acknowledge and endure what is otherwise unendurable."

Humor is certainly a help and a key in dealing with our everyday problems and distresses. It keeps us focused on our priorities, and keeps us open to the workings of the Spirit who provides guidance and direction for us.

As we continue to look, first to Christ and the cross, and then to our problems and frustrations, we are enabled to deal with them more appropriately.

A man jumped from an airplane and pulled the ripcord of his parachute. Nothing happened. He pulled the ripcord on his emergency chute, and still nothing happened. Plummeting toward the ground, he saw a woman hurtling up toward him.

"Do you know anything about ripcords?" the man shouted.

"No," replied the woman. "Do you know anything about gas stoves?"

Reflections

1. Discuss with a friend ways that you use humor to deal with the hurts and pains in your life.

2. Search the Scriptures to find words of comfort and peace in times of trouble. Experience the hope we have in our Lord.

NOT PERFECT, BUT GREAT

Here is a story that depicts the joy we have in a loving Lord who forgives and keeps us going in life. See how it connects with your life today.

The wedding was planned to be a perfect one. Everything was set. The flowers were beautiful. The bride was stunning. The music was flawless. The ring bearer even had his hair combed. Everything was going well—until the recessional began. Uncle Harry, unbeknownst to anyone, was planning to set off some fireworks as the bridal party marched out of church. What a perfect end to a perfect ceremony, he thought. However, just as he was lighting the surprise, he accidentally hit the board on which the fireworks were mounted. Instead of directing the fireworks out over the church parking lot, they were now turned to go directly at the happy bridal party.

What looked like the perfect wedding, wasn't anymore. But, it sure became a great wedding! For the video camera man not only filmed the service, but also got the special effects of fireworks zooming in on the wedding party! And, it was great! Not perfect anymore, but great! Folks are still enjoying watching the video of that great wedding, especially the fireworks!

And that is how our lives go too. Not perfect, but great. We still get messed up with problems in our lives. Things still don't go the way we wish. And so our daily living is not perfect, but it sure is great, because of the presence and comfort and hope of our Lord in our lives. The Lord of Life continues to move and direct and forgive us so that our lives become exciting and great, even

though far from perfect.

So, how is your job going? Not perfect, but great, because of the presence of the Lord.

So how are your relationships with family and friends going? Not perfect, but great, because of our Lord's promise to us.

So, how is your life going? Not perfect, but great, because of Christ's death and resurrection for each of us.

Not perfect, but great. That's good enough for me. And now, let's continue the fireworks!

Reflections

1. What things in your life are not perfect, but great, because of the Lord's presence?

2. What type of fireworks in your life have caused excitement, turmoil, and struggles?

DEPENDING ON THE LORD

A man was hanging from a cliff a thousand feet above the ground. He was frightened and petrified and screamed, "Is there anyone up there who can help me?"

Just then he heard a big booming voice from above that said, "Yes, I will help you. I am the Lord. Just relax and let go." There was a long pause.

"Is there anyone else up there who can help me?"

Letting go is never easy. And it is also easy to begin depending on ourselves, our good health, and even on our positive attitude and sense of humor, instead of depending on the Lord Himself. Our dependence on Him allows us to use the gifts He has given us, rather than the other way around. So, what do you need to let go of, in order to focus on the Lord's hold on you? Maybe it is our strong interest in pleasing everyone, or our intent on having the happiest and best family, job, spouse (add your own to the list).

"Is there anyone up there who can help me?" There certainly is, and the good news is that He is not just "up there." He is right here with us now, to love, forgive, and be our constant source of help.

Let go, and let God!

Reflections

1. When burdened and worried, to what or whom do you turn for help and comfort?

2. How does the Lord use people around you to comfort and support you?

RELIEF

How do you spell RELIEF?
One way to spell it is L-A-U-G-H-T-E-R.

Consider the following description of a physical reaction:

The neural circuits in your brain begin to reverberate. Chemical and electrical impulses start flowing rapidly through your body. The pituitary gland is stimulated; hormones and endorphins race through your blood. Your body temperature rises half a degree, your pulse rate and blood pressure increase, your arteries and thoracic muscles contract, your vocal chords quiver, and your face contorts. Pressure builds in your lungs. Your lower jaw suddenly becomes uncontrollable, and breath bursts from your mouth at nearly 70 miles an hour.

We have just described laughter from a clinical point of view. It sounds more like a disease, but it does point out that laughter involves the entire body.

More and more studies continue to point out that laughter is good for us, that it relieves tension and reduces stress, not to mention all of the social and spiritual benefits it brings.

Norman Cousins' landmark book *Anatomy of an Illness* certainly heightened the awareness of the value of laughter on the body. Cousins stated that he "made the joyous discovery that 10 minutes of genuine belly laughter had an anesthetic effect and would give me at least two hours of pain-free sleep . . . I was greatly elated that there is a physiologic basis for the ancient theory that laughter is good medicine."

It does need to be pointed out that laughter does not cure disease, nor will it put a person in a right relationship with the Lord. The fact that Cousins died a few years ago, even with all of his studies on the value of laughter again makes this clear. Only the Lord Himself, through His life, death, and resurrection is victorious over death.

C-H-R-I-S-T is the only true way of spelling R-E-L-I-E-F.

Reflections

1. Check out other resources regarding the connection between humor and illness. It is a fascinating area of study.

2. Do some regular good old belly laughs every day, with or without people present, and check how your body and mind react to this inner jogging.

OUT OF THE MOUTHS

Isn't it fun to see and hear how little children, full of vigor and pep, portray their humor as they attempt to respond to an adult world and their faith? Some children shared the following answers to questions. As you review them, note what it is that makes their responses humorous.

Noah's wife was called Joan of Arc.

The Fifth Commandment is "Humor thy father and mother."

When Mary heard she was to be the mother of Jesus, she went out and sang the Magna Carta.

Christians have only one wife. This is called monotony.

The plane that brought Jesus to Egypt was flown by Pontius the Pilot.

It is sometimes difficult to hear in church because the agnostics are so terrible.

These responses show that humor is close to reality. We find something humorous when it "smells real" and "hits the mark." We thank the Lord for little kids who keep us adults humble in our humor. We thank the Lord for the happy faith of little ones who teach us something about life and faith each day.

Reflections

1. Listen for other responses of children at home and in worship and Sunday school. Write them down and share them, in love, with others.

2. What can we adults learn from these and other responses?

HUMOR COMMUNICATES, PART I

"To communicate, get them laughing!"

Someone must have said that, since it is so true. People of all ages tend to listen and learn if they are laughing and waiting for the surprises of a presentation, story, or conversation. Watch and study some of the better preachers or presenters or actors. They have a way of capturing the audience through personal interest stories and anecdotes.

To illustrate, a story (what else!):

The village blacksmith hired a young man who was eager to learn the trade. The blacksmith wanted to train the new helper well, so he started with these instructions:

"Now listen carefully and do exactly as I say. When I take the hot iron from the fire, I'll place it on the anvil; then when I nod my head, you strike it with this hammer."

The young man did exactly as he was told, according to his understanding. Now he's the new village blacksmith!

Take a look at the Lord and how He communicated to the people around Him. He caught their attention, He responded to their needs, He sensed their interests and used everyday signs and visuals to make His point.

And He still does this with us today. He provides the gifts of communication and humor and understanding in order to allow us, as His people, to effectively communicate the joy and peace we have, as His people!

Reflections

1. Watch for examples of humorous stories used in sermons and other presentations. What effects do they have on the listeners?

2. As you speak to others try to use real-life humorous stories.

HUMOR COMMUNICATES, PART II

Remember this statement? "I know you believe you understand what you think I said, but I am not sure you realize that what you heard is not what I meant!"

Humor does communicate. Try this one on for size:

A district school executive told his assistant executive: "Next Thursday at 10:30 A.M., Halley's comet will appear over this area. This is an event which occurs only once every 75 years. Call the school principals and have them assemble their teachers and classes on their athletic fields and explain this phenomenon to them. It if rains, then cancel the day's observation and have the classes meet in the auditorium to see a film about the comet."

Here's what the assistant said to school principals: "By order of the school executive, next

Thursday at 10:30, Halley's comet will appear over your athletic field. If it rains, then cancel the day's classes and report to the auditorium with your teachers and students, where you will be shown films, a phenomenal event which occurs once every 75 years."

And the principals to the teachers: "By order of the phenomenal district school executive, at 10:30 next Thursday, Halley's comet will appear in the auditorium. In case of rain over the athletic field, the executive will give another order, something which occurs once every 75 years."

Teachers to students: "Next Thursday at 10:30, the school executive will appear in our school auditorium with Halley's comet, something which occurs every 75 years. If it rains, the executive will cancel the comet and order us all out to our phenomenal athletic field."

Students to parents: "When it rains next Thursday at 10:30 over the school athletic field, the phenomenal 75-year-old school executive will cancel all classes and appear before the whole school in the auditorium, accompanied by Bill Haley and the Comets!"

Reflections

1. Think of instances in Scripture where the people listening to Jesus did not understand what he was saying or at least did not comprehend His complete message.

2. What are ways that you can improve your communication skills and use of words in order to communicate more effectively?

WE ARE THE PEOPLE OF GOD

Colossians 3:12–17 says it so well. "You are the people of God; He loved you and chose you for His own."

And then St. Paul continues by affirming the gifts that we have been given as we live out the fact that God has made us His people. We are enabled by Him to show compassion, kindness, patience, humility, and thanksgiving. We are enabled to live a life of joyful celebration, not because we use these gifts well, but because God has called us to be His people.

Isn't it great that we do not have to do it ourselves? The Lord does not say, "Use your gifts, be happy, try harder, and, if you succeed, then I'll let you be one of mine!" Instead, He affirms in us that we already are His, because of what Christ has done for us, and therefore we have the power to live a sanctified life of caring and concern for others.

And the gifts of joy and celebration fit right in. We are the people of God! And that makes all the difference in the world. Let's make all the difference in the world by living this calling out, in a world that so desperately needs joy and celebration.

Reflections

1. How does it make you feel to know that "you are a person of God"—now, always, forever?

2. How do you plan to go about telling other people that they are His people also?

THE GRAND PARENTHESIS

Easter people live in the hope and joy of the resurrection!

Conrad Hyers, in *And God Created Laughter*, explains that Easter people live in the "grand parenthesis" within which Jesus' ministry took place.

Christ's ministry began with the joyful annunciation to Mary and the angelic alleluias of His birth. It ended with the ascension and the birth of the church on Pentecost.

In between are disappointment, rejection, conflict, sorrow, suffering, and death. Yet the overarching context remains one of celebration and joy.

The first and last words belong not to death but to life, not to sorrow but to joy, not to weeping but to laughter.

We, too, are called to live in this parenthesis. We live, not in the context of Good Friday and the crucifixion, but in the context of Easter and Pentecost. And as pain and sorrow and death continue in our lives, we know in faith that "death has been swallowed up in victory" (1 Cor. 15:54, NIV).

Jesus' ministry begins in celebration. His ministry continues in Easter celebration through our daily lives of joy and in our living out the "grand parenthesis!"

Let's get on with the celebration!

Reflections

1. Share with someone some of the Good Friday experiences in your life.

2. Also share with someone some of your Easter, good news experiences!

EASIER OR EASTER?

Lord, make my life easier.

Perhaps you have prayed a prayer similar to this too. I have. Lord, can't you ease up a little? Can't you make a few things go well, or at least better than before? Why, Lord, does this always happen to me?

Lord, make my life easier!

And He does. In His own way and on His own schedule. The Lord does it simply by changing the word "easier" into the word "Easter"! Because of Easter, we can now pray instead, "Lord, make my life Easter!"

And He does it by simply substituting the *i* in easier for the *t* in Easter. All the *i*'s in my life are replaced by the *t* of the cross.

Lord, thanks for making my life Easter! And help others to see Easter through me!

Reflections

1. When do you most often pray, "Lord, make my life easier"? Reflect on some of your down times.

2. When do you pray "Lord, make my life Easter"? Again, share these thoughts with a friend.

READY, WILLING, AND ENABLED

Don Wharton has a song out entitled "Ready, Willing, and Enabled." What a great title for a song, and what a great slogan for our life together in the Lord.

Romans 5:1–5 tells us all about God readying us for ministry.

We *are* ready because of God's act in Christ to redeem us. We *are* willing, because of the power of the Spirit in us. And we *are* enabled by our Baptism to reach out and share this joy with others around us.

But sometimes we act as though we are *not* ready, willing, and enabled to accomplish the Lord's tasks. We become so wrapped up in ourselves, we concentrate on what's right for us rather than ministering to people around us.

And then we hear God's word of love and forgiveness. We hear St. Paul shouting out to us that "God has poured out His love into our hearts by means of the Holy Spirit, who is God's gift to us" (Rom. 5:5). And we once again become ready, willing, and enabled! That's the joy we have to share. That's why we can laugh at our foolishness and move on to care for and love others.

Ready, willing, and enabled—that's us! Because of the enabling power of the Spirit who gets us ready and willing, in Jesus' name!

Reflections

1. When do you not feel ready, or willing, to minister to others?
2. When do you feel ready, willing, and enabled? What makes the difference?

TAKING THE RISK

A man hated cats. His wife owned a cat. One day he decided to get rid of the cat and not tell his wife. In fact, after the cat disappeared, the man put up signs all over the neighborhood offering a $1,000 reward for anyone who could find and return his wife's cat. One of his neighbors stopped him one day and complimented him on his commitment and willingness to find his wife's cat. To that, the man simply said, "When you know what I know, you can afford to take the risk!"

In a real sense, we, too, are people who can take risks in our lives, because of what we know! We know that Christ has died and risen again for us! We know that He loves us now and will love us forever. We know that He has prepared a place for us in eternal heaven. We are risk-takers, because of what we know!

So we can risk celebrating life, even in the midst of pain and suffering. We can risk spending time and energy for other people. We can risk becoming a servant for others, because of Christ the Servant.

Let's continue to take risks for others, because of what we know.

And, more importantly, because of Whom we know!

Reflections

1. What are some risks you can take in your life, right now?

2. Name some people you know whom you have an opportunity to love and serve, even if it means taking some risks.

TRUSTING
IN THE LORD

"God is to be trusted, the God who called you to have fellowship with His Son Jesus Christ, our Lord" (1 Cor. 1:9). Whom do you trust? The Lord, of course. Why do we ask? I trust in the Lord, too, some of the time. But sometimes I find myself trusting in myself, or someone else, or in my accomplishments, or health, or well-being, or future, rather than first trusting in the Lord and seeing all of these other situations in life as gifts from Him. And maybe you do also. We trust in a Lord who is trustworthy. He has never let us down, nor will He ever let us down. That is the one thing in life that is not going to change!

And that is reason for joy and smiles. And that is worth telling others about. And when we fail to trust, and fall back into our old patterns, the Lord continues to be there to woo us back and to provide His trusting love to us once again.

We can learn trust from our friend Anthony Clancy. Clancy was an Irishman for whom the number seven cropped up with inordinate regularity in his life. He was the seventh child of a seventh child. He was born on the seventh day of the week, on the seventh day of the month, in the seventh month of the year, in the seventh year of the century. On his 27th birthday he went to a racetrack where he discovered that the seventh horse in the seventh race was named Seventh

Heaven. Its running weight was seven stone, and its odds were seven to one. Thinking this was all too good to be true, Clancy confidently bet seven shillings on the horse.

And it came in seventh!

Reflections

1. What things have you trusted in that have let you down in the past?

2. Think of an acquaintance who trusts in something or someone other than the Lord. How can you share God's love and care with that person?

THE USE OF TIME

I have decided never to say "I just don't have time to do that" again. We all have 24 hours each day to accomplish many things. When I do not do something, it is not because I didn't have time. It is because I did not take the time to do it. There were other things, for whatever reason, that got in the way of my accomplishing something.

Time is a gift from God, and as we sometimes misuse His other gifts, we sure can misuse our time. But a healthy outlook allows us to sort through and evaluate how we can best use our time. *Time management* is not as important as *life management*, the priorities we set for the gift of time.

Stress has been defined as "What happens when your gut says no and your mouth says, 'Of course, I'd be glad to'!" How true, how true! I have not yet found the perfect schedule to make use of time, but I am getting closer to realizing that my time needs to be spent in a variety of ways—in structured ways; in personal, private ways; for physical exercise; for study and devotion; for preparation; for family and friends; and for care and service to others.

One of the best ways to sort our priorities on time is to learn how to say no more often than yes. In so doing, we will be saying yes to more effective use of our time.

Reflections

1. How do you feel about your use of time? What would you like to have more time to do? What can you say no to in order to have more time for yes in your schedule?

2. Chart for one week how you use your time—include sleeping, eating, visiting, working, playing, doing nothing. How does the way you spend your time reflect the priorities in your life?

HE'S ONE OF YOU

In her children's book, *The Mysterious Star* (Concordia, 1974), Joanne Marxhausen tells the story of a young boy who longs to see Jesus' Christmas star. Jamie's father tells him, "You'll find the star, but not in the sky."

Jamie does not understand, but as he sets off to search for the star, he stops to share Jesus' love with a sad little girl, to offer a peanut-butter-and-jelly sandwich to a lonely old man, to give a drink of water to a tired newspaper boy, and to help everyone else in his path who needs some comfort. When Jamie sadly tells his father that he could not find the star, his dad wonders who all these friends are that followed him home. Jamie turns to see everyone who followed him, and they explain how they saw the star shining in him as he shared Jesus' love.

We, too, can help spread the news that Christ shines in each of us; that we are created in the likeness of God (James 3:9). We love Christ when we love each other. What a marvelous way to live! Christ indeed lives in us.

"What a friend we have in Jesus," we sing. And what a Jesus we have in friends!

A little boy was watching the famous sculptor Michelangelo work on his statue of David. Each day the little lad came and watched the artist at work, and every day the boy said nothing. He just stood there gazing at the artist.

Finally, after months of sculpting, Michelangelo was ready to unveil his masterpiece, a white marble boy David. As he did, the crowd oo-oohed and ah-h-hed, but the boy still said nothing. Finally the little guy came up to the artist, tugged at him and said, "Hey, how'd you know he was in there?" And that's the question people ask of us. How do they know the Lord Jesus Christ is alive in us? We answer that query by responding to them in love and care and hope.

Christ dwells in us! We are the temple of the Holy Spirit! And that makes us special!

Reflections

1. When do you most feel the presence of the Lord in your life?

2. How can you reach out more intentionally to others to show them that the Lord is within you, loving and motivating you for service?

ANGELS CAN FLY

Aren't you glad angels can fly because they take themselves lightly? Me too!

And aren't you also glad that we are free to fly and celebrate in Christ because He has taken our heavy sin upon Himself on the cross so that we can take ourselves lightly? Me too! Life is not one big, happy party of continual bliss and laughter. Sin is still very much in the picture. But the victory over sin has freed us to live in joy and eternal hope. That's why we can fly. That's why we continue the celebration, even in the midst of the world's pain and problems.

And now our task is to move out and share our victory in Christ with others. And what a joy-filled task it is, because the Lord has had the last laugh. He has won. The victory is ours.

And so fly, my friends, fly. Fly as you share and celebrate and serve. Fly as you laugh and cry with each other. Fly as you join together in singing and shouting with all the angels, archangels, and the whole company of heaven. Fly as we sing and shout together, "I know that my Redeemer lives!"

We can fly! We can sing! We can celebrate! Because God has done it all for us!

And I'm glad!

Reflections

1. What two things can you begin to do differently in your life right now, in order to show that you can fly?

2. Which two people can you zero in on to help see the joy of the Lord so that they can join you in your flights?

PARTY TIME

It doesn't take some people long to realize that many adults (and youth, too) have become too serious, too tense, too stressed-out. We have taken life and ourselves too seriously. And it could be that the older we get the more difficult it is to enjoy life—although I have met some excellent exceptions to this.

Rabbi Edward Cohen describes life like this: "Life is tough. It takes up a lot of your time, all your weekends, and what do you get in the end? . . . I think that the life cycle is all backwards. You should die first, get it out of the way. Then you live 20 years in an old-age home. You get kicked out when you're too young. You get a gold watch. You go to work. You work 40 years until you're young enough to enjoy your retirement. You go to college. You party until you're ready for high school. You go to grade school. You become a little kid. You play. You have no responsibilities. You become a little baby. You go back into the womb. You spend your last months floating. And you finish up as a gleam in somebody's eye."

What has happened to that gleam in someone's eye? What has happened to the joyful, fun-loving spirit we once had? Mike Yaconelli, of Youth Specialties, says that "the childlikeness in all of us gets snuffed out over the years. This society has put out the 'light in men's souls'."

The more pagan a society gets, the more boring its people become. We still have a light on in our souls! We still have a gleam in our eyes, because Jesus is in our hearts. We are alive, never boring, always playful, exhibiting in our everydayness the "spunk" of the Spirit.

This light in us, that allows us to take life lightly, is the spontaneous light of Jesus Christ Himself! As Mike continues, "Christians are not just people who live godly lives. We are people who know how to live—period! Christians are not just examples of moral piety. We are people filled with a bold mischievousness of the Gospel! Christians not only know how to live pure lives, we also know how to party!"

Yes, it is time for a party. This party started at the foot of the cross, moved to the empty tomb, and traveled through history as the Spirit motivated His people to live lightly and celebratively throughout the years.

Let the party continue! Christ lives! And so do we!

Reflections

1. What are some reasons, do you suppose, that the Christian church is still seen by many as a place of somber seriousness instead of a place of celebration and joy?

2. What can you, your family, your church do to turn life into one big celebration?

SO WHAT?

What difference has this book made in you?

This is a question only you can answer, but I hope that through this sharing, you have caught and captured and experienced some of the joy of the Gospel that is ours in Christ!

I also hope that you picked up one or two new stories and illustrations that you can use. And I certainly hope that it has been a fun experience for you as you reflect on your life of joy and hope in the days ahead.

Thanks for sharing your time with me. I look forward to more exciting times with you and other people of God, either here on this globe, or certainly in eternity with you.

Until then, keep flying . . . and do take yourself lightly!

BIBLIOGRAPHY

Bimler, Rich. *Celebrating Saints*. St. Louis: Concordia Publishing House, 1986.

Bonham, Tal D. *Humor: God's Gift*. Nashville: Broadman Press, 1988.

Cote, Richard. *Holy Mirth: A Theology of Laughter*. Whitinsville: Affirmation Books, 1985.

Cousins, Norman. *Anatomy of an Illness As Perceived by the Patient: Reflections on Healing and Regeneration*. New York: W. W. Norton and Company, 1979.

Erickson, Kenneth. *The Power of Praise*. St. Louis: Concordia Publishing House, 1984.

Hyers, Conrad. *And God Created Laughter: The Bible As Divine Comedy*. Louisville: Westminster John Knox Press, 1987.

The Joyful Noiseletter. Monthly newsletter of the Fellowship of Merry Christians, Cal Samra, P. O. Box 668, Kalamazoo, MI 49005.

Kane, Thomas A. *Happy Are You Who Affirm*. Whitinsville: Affirmation Books, 1980.

Laughing Matters. Humor Project, Sagamore Institute, 110 Spring Street, Saratoga Springs, NY 12866

Maycroft, Leslie. "Humor in the Classroom." Lutheran Education Association Monograph, 1990.

Peck, M. Scott. *The Different Drum: Community Making and Peace*. New York: Simon and Schuster, Inc., 1987.

Peter, Laurence J. and Bill Dana. *The Laughter Prescription*. New York: Ballantine Books, Inc., 1982.

Prelutsky, Jack. *New Kid on the Block*. New York: Greenwillow Books, 1984.

Samra, Cal. *The Joyful Christ: The Healing Power of Humor.* Harper & Row, 1986.

Sheehy, Gail. *Pathfinders.* New York: Bantam Books, 1982.

Trueblood, Elton. *The Humor of Christ.* New York: Harper & Row Publishers, Inc., 1975.

Willimon, William H. *And the Laugh Shall Be First: A Treasury of Religious Humor.* Nashville: Abingdon Press, 1986.